Positively Upbeat!

featuring Auntie P

52914

by Patricia Kearney

Illustrations by Dexter Santos

"People deal too much with the negative, with what is wrong. Why not try and see positive things, to just touch those things and make them bloom?"

THÍCH NHẤT HẠNH, VIETNAMESE POET, ZEN BUDDHIST MONK, TEACHER, AUTHOR, POET, AND PEACE ACTIVIST

"Formulate and stamp indelibly on your mind a mental picture of yourself as succeeding. Hold this picture tenaciously. Never permit it to fade. Your mind will seek to develop the picture... Do not build up obstacles in your imagination."

NORMAN VINCENT PEALE, MINISTER AND AUTHOR (MAY 31, 1898 – DECEMBER 24, 1993)

"Open Mind – be open to new experiences and new ideas, always keep a sense of wonder and remember that anything is possible."

PATRICK SUSOEFF, COMPOSER (OPEN EARS, OPEN MIND, OPEN HEART, BY P.SUS)

DEDICATION

I dedicate this book to all those who are in the habit of accentuating the positive. What fun it is to enjoy a positive life. Pass it on!

Connolly, Hayes & Heffernan Publishers
P. O. Box 40322
Pittsburgh, PA 15201
www.auntiep.com

Editor: Sydnee Bagovich

Positively Upbeat! First Edition, October 27, 2014
ISBN: 978-0-615-81086-7

Cataloging-in-Publication Data
Library of Congress Control Number: 2013907946

Positively Upbeat! \Kearney-McCarty, Patricia

Thanks to: The Veronas – Danni, Mike, Bryce, Brody, Brynne and Kael, Family Martial Arts Academy (Beaverton, Oregon), Rabbi Elimelech Goldberg (Kids Kicking Cancer – http://kidskickingcancer.org/content/our-program/), Mark and Aly Smith, The Boilermaker Jazz Band, Kevin and Aubry Copeland, Ernst (www.mccartyart.com), Carolann Cioffi DeSantis, Frank Andrews, Soo Clark, and thanks especially to Jane Jacobson, the most "positively upbeat" person I know.

Illustrations: Dexter Santos
Design: Paulette Green, P Green Design
Photo back cover: Michele D'Emo

Auntie P always travels by train, with her suitcase and dancing shoes.

She loves dancing, traveling, and visiting her family. This time she is visiting with her nephew, Kael, and is going to stay at Kael's grandparents' house in Oregon. Auntie P can't wait to see everyone after her spectacular ride on the scenic train. Kael's grandmother and grandfather have come to pick her up at the station.

"Oh, it's so good to be here and see you all," says Auntie P, greeting everyone. "On my way from the Medford swing dance event, I thought I would take the Oregon scenic train! What a wonderful experience. It was something I wanted to do all my life. There were gigantic windows on the train to view the beautiful scenery along the way. I had a perfect window seat and was able to take photos."

"I went to the swing dance at the Evergreen Ball Room," beams Auntie P. "My dance lessons were so much fun! The Boilermaker Jazz Band was performing there, so I just had to go! Everybody dances. We get to change partners, so we can learn different styles. Everyone gets the chance to make new friends."

Everyone dances!

"What's been going on with everyone?" asks Auntie P. Brynne, Kael's sister, can't wait to tell Auntie P the neighborhood news. "We're having a fundraiser for the local puppy shelter in two days," announces Brynne. "I'm so excited about it I can hardly sit still. Do you remember that I told you I wanted to study theatre when I go to college? Well, organizing the fundraiser has shown me that I can handle it all. I am the producer, stage manager, and the director, Auntie P. It's positively fabulous!" exclaims Brynne.

"I'm having jugglers, ballerinas, kids singing, pet tricks, a food stand, and handmade items for sale," Brynne tells Auntie P. "All of our efforts will go toward the puppy shelter. Do you have something you can do, Auntie P? It's for a good cause."

"Let me think about this, Brynne," says Auntie P. "Maybe I could exhibit my fencing poses. Can you believe it? I'm learning how to fence!"

"Where is Kael?" asks Auntie P. "He's outside in the rose garden," replies Kael's dad. "He's been asking for you all day." "Thanks again for allowing me to visit," laughs Auntie P. "I enjoy my train rides and getting to see you all. It surely helps to keep me upbeat!" "Oh, Auntie P," says Grandma, "Kael would be so happy to hear all about your trip on the train. He just loves trains!"

"Hi, Kael and Kevin!" yells Auntie P. "I'm here at last. How are you boys doing?" Kael is running away from a bird flying around the garden. "I don't like this bird swooping down on me!" Kael yells back to Auntie P. "Why won't he just go away!"

"Oh, my," says Auntie P, "you seem to have made a new friend! Slow down. Let him perch on your arm. He won't hurt you, I'm sure. Stay calm and don't run!"

Kael stops running from the bird and gives Auntie P a grand hug. "Hello, Auntie P," says Kael. "My friend Kevin and I are so glad to finally see you." Kael loves calling Aunt Patricia by her nickname, *Auntie P*. It makes him giggle inside.

"I really don't like birds flying near me, Auntie P," says Kael. "I'm not afraid, but I don't want the bird to pull my hair or rip my shirt," sighs Kael. "You need to be calm, Kael," says Auntie P. "Talk to the little bird. He may want to give you a sweet little message in your ear." "Oh, no, Auntie P," replies Kael. "I don't want that bird near *my* ear!"

"You need to accentuate the positive, Kael. Try to make it a habit of being more positive, right, Kevin?" says Auntie P. "What's a habit, Auntie P?" asks Kael. "Kevin and I don't know what that means." "We're just kids," remarks Kevin. Kael nods his head in agreement.

"You are right, Kevin. I will try to explain," says Auntie P.

"You make your bed every day, right?" asks Auntie P. "You make your bed and you brush your teeth. You don't even think about it. It's something you do every day. Well, that's a habit."

"When I wake up each day and make my bed," continues Auntie P, "I always tell myself that the new day will be fun. That's being positive. It's thinking that today is going to be a great day. When that little bird flies toward you the next time, maybe you should greet it with open arms and a smile instead of running away."

"I'm willing to try, Auntie P," says Kevin. "I'll try to figure out what being positive is. Let's try it, Kael. Forget about the bird." "OK, Kevin," replies Kael. "I'll give it a go. I will try....and I'll smile."

Kael tells Auntie P about the fundraiser for the puppy shelter this weekend. "Some kids are dancing, juggling, making crafts, or singing," Kael says. "When I sing, I sometimes don't know the right words yet. The kids might laugh at me." "Let's think of something we can do," says Kevin. "Maybe your dad could help us." "That sounds like a great idea, Kevin," says Auntie P. "Be positive!"

Auntie P is happy to see one of her favorite neighbors in the back yard. "Hi, Aly! It's so nice to see you. What have you been doing lately?" asks Auntie P. "I haven't spoken to you since my last visit to Portland."

"I've designed costumes for the fundraiser show," replies Aly. "I'm also going to have a macramé stand and raise money from the things I've designed! Here are some samples, Auntie P."

"My, my, Aly, you create such beautiful things. You design in twos! Everything is two—two belts, two hats, two vests. That's remarkable." "Oh, I can't help it, Auntie P," says Aly. I always make two of everything. Speaking of two, the fundraiser is in TWO days! I need to have everything ready."

"Do you remember Mark, Auntie P? He's my best, best friend in the world," giggles Aly. "He lives down the block from my house. He's the nicest person you'd ever want to know."

FOOD
by Mark

- Sandwiches with or without pickles
- Lemonade
- Iced Tea

"Mark has a special skill, Auntie P," says Aly. "Oh, really, and what is that?" asks Auntie P. "He can smell sandwiches," Aly tells Auntie P, with great pride. "That certainly is very special, Aly," replies Auntie P. "It is special, Auntie P," says Aly. "He not only smells a sandwich, but he can tell you what kind of bread it's on...like if it's on rye with seeds, mustard, mayo or maybe has a pickle! Isn't that cool?"

"Well, if it's that specific, then I guess it is positively special, and could come in handy some day," says Auntie P with a laugh.

"Kael, have you thought more about what you can do for the puppy shelter fundraiser?" asks Auntie P. "Yes. My dad has been teaching me Karate, Auntie P," says Kael. "He's an expert. He said he would give me Karate lessons every day, and he really does! He said we could give an exhibition on the stage of what we've learned. I think we should. That's positive, right, Auntie P?"

"Why, yes it is. It's great that you and your dad thought of doing this, Kael," says Auntie P with joy. "It's very special." "I'm learning the martial art of Karate, too, Auntie P," chimes in Kevin.

"Every day we learn something new in Karate,"
says Kael's dad. "I'm so happy, Kael and Kevin, that you
are interested in learning. I can see that it's a wonderful
and positive experience for you. I've been practicing the
art of Karate for years myself and always have more to
learn and strive for. You kids are getting in the habit of
doing a little bit each day." "Oh, we know what a habit
is, Dad," says Kael. "Auntie P told us all about it."

"This is great!" says Auntie P. "I will do my fencing. It will be such fun, doing my fencing poses! I can't believe that I'm going to be on the stage in two days showing everyone what I've learned. En Garde! Thrust! Pare! Disengage!" shouts Auntie P, moving around the yard with grace and style in her fencing outfit and mask.

The day of the event has arrived. Everyone is so excited. *The House is open,* announces Brynne. All the neighbors are filing into the seating area and taking their places to watch the performances on stage. Afterward, they will all go to Aly's exhibit and get a bite to eat at Mark's food stand.

"Mark, is your stand ready for customers after the show?" asks Brynne. "Oh, yes, Brynne, I have everything ready!" answers Mark. "Ballerinas, please be on stage in three minutes. Cue the music!" directs Brynne, with a huge smile.

The first performers are the adorable ballerinas twirling in their lovely costumes. They look so lovely. Everyone in the audience claps with great enthusiasm. The ballerinas are followed by the jugglers, who are also wearing colorful outfits. Auntie P shows everyone what she's learned about the art of fencing. She makes sure to tell everyone about rules she learned in the beginner classes. Learning about safety is very important in any activity, including biking, swimming, and jumping rope.

Next, everyone sees Kael, Kevin, and Kael's dad exhibiting the martial art of Karate. "Horse Stance!" requests Kael's dad on stage. Kael's dad tells everyone that learning the martial art of Karate helps to develop stronger focus, concentration, and self-discipline skills. He tells everyone how important it is to observe good manners. "We always bow to show our respect and to demonstrate that we are calm, and practice in a safe way."

The neighbors are excited to see the exhibition and enjoy how well the boys have learned their skills. The show ends on a positive note, with great applause from the whole audience.

Auntie P asks Aubry, Kevin's sister, if she liked seeing the show. "I loved every minute, Auntie P," says Aubry. "I loved the ballerinas and their costumes. I hope that Aly will make me a pretty tutu one day! I love dancing." "Well, it seems like the fundraiser is a great success," says Auntie P. "You kids did so much to help all those adorable puppies. It's time to celebrate!"

"Let's kick up our heels," says Auntie P. "Let's celebrate by doing the *Positively Upbeat!* Anyone interested?" "Oh, boy, Auntie P, I think I smell a roast turkey on whole wheat...with mustard," says Mark. "I'll check if there's a pickle!"

"Don't mind Mark, Auntie P," chuckles Aly. "He's not much of a dancer." "Let's just do it, then," sings Auntie P. "It's really Simple Dimple! Positively! Let's go, kids!"

Shake your hands to the sky...

"I think I get it now, Auntie P," giggles Kael. "I can learn to do lots of new things and smile at the same time. I'm in the habit and POSITIVE!"

"Gettin' down with the beat, Gettin' down, move our feet! U-P-B-E-A-T..."

Lyrics for Positively Upbeat!

Gettin' down with the beat
Gettin' down, move your feet
Gettin' down is
Positively Upbeat!

Shake your hands to the sky
Bend your knees, clap and slide
Gettin' down is
Positively Upbeat!

U –P - B – E – A – T   upbeat
U –P - B – E – A – T   Positively Upbeat!

Positively Upbeat!
Lyrics: Patricia Kearney
Music: Ernest McCarty, Jr.
2014 ©KearPublisha Musik – BMI

Music for Positively Upbeat!

Positively Upbeat!
Lyrics: Patricia Kearney
Music: Ernest McCarty, Jr.
2014 ©KearPublisha Musik – BMI

artist
Dexter Santos

Dexter Santos has been drawing ever since he was three years old. His fascination with art started with the comic books he read and collected as well as the children's books that stimulated his imagination as a kid. All throughout his elementary and high school years, Dexter participated in any event that had anything to do with drawing or painting and won for himself a handful of awards that further encouraged his artwork.

Continuing his passion for art as an adult, Dexter has seen his artwork manifested in art shows, on postcards, t-shirts, the internet, the back of a bus, and even projected on a movie theater screen. As an illustrator for children's books, Dexter is excited and honored to tell the story of Auntie P and the wonderful life lessons she imparts on young children.

Dexter has a BFA in Character Animation and Visual Effects from the Academy of Art University in San Francisco and currently resides in Seattle, Washington, where you'll most likely find him in cafes and bookstores indulging his artistic activities and introvert side. Aside from being an artist, Dexter is also a nationally renowned Blues dance teacher and dancer. In his spare time, he likes to social dance, sing, play his ukulele, and go on afternoon motorcycle rides.

Find out more about Dexter's artwork at **dexterityink.com** and his dancing at **dextersantos.com.**

Dedication

This book is dedicated to the memory of my grandmother, Pacienciosa Flores who had a warm, kind, and generous heart and whose love for her family was unwavering. She always stayed positive despite life's adversities, and shared her warm smile and calm demeanor with those around her. Though you are sorely missed, I will always remember you and your love, Lola.

—DEXTER SANTOS

Patricia Kearney, born in Brooklyn, New York, and raised on Long Island, resides with her husband in New York City and in Lawrenceville, Pennsylvania. Her background experience includes producing in off-Broadway theatre and the music business. *Positively Upbeat!* is the third in her series of books featuring Auntie P. Unlike Auntie P, who "always travels by train," Ms. Kearney travels all over the world in trains, planes, boats, autos, and also the occasional jaunting cart—especially when vacationing in the Republic of Ireland, the town of Carrick-on-Suir in Co. Tipperary being one of her favorites!

Ms. Kearney is married to playwright, director, composer, sculptor and visual artist, Ernest McCarty, Jr., of Chicago.

Other books *featuring Auntie P*

by Patricia Kearney

www.auntiep.com

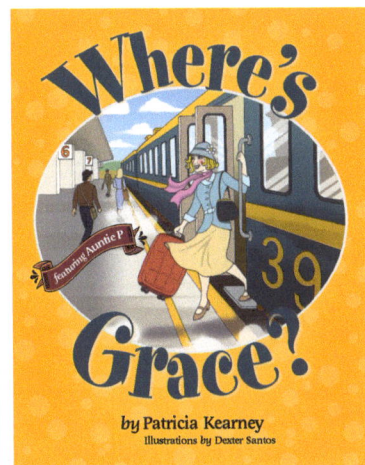

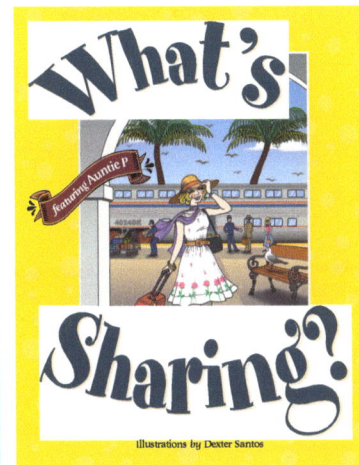

Where's Grace!
by Patricia Kearney
Illustrations by Dexter Santos

What's Sharing?
Illustrations by Dexter Santos

Winner of GDUSA's American Graphic Design Award – Certificate of Excellence